POWERHOUSE DIALING
SCRIPT BOOK

BY: ANDY HERRINGTON

ISBN-13: 978-0-9920326-1-6

Published By:
Powerhouse Coaching Publications
Whitby, Ontario, Canada

Scripting seems to be an evil word in many circles, but I know that whether or not you realize it, you are using a script each and every time you are on the phone. Over the days, weeks, months and years you have learnt what works and what doesn't and have formed some version of a script. What is really in debate is the extent of the script, how exact you are each and every time and who wrote the script. Personally, I have used other people's scripts and have written my own. The results have varied and not in the way many people would like to believe. Neither the 'do you own thing' nor the 'My script is the only right script' people will be happy when I say that I have had equal success from both version and equal failures from both versions.

What I have found is that there are five truisms to scripting no matter what you do, or where you are and I'd like to share them with you.

A script written down is far better than one in your head.
Once you write something down, you can set about a. learning it word for word and b. improving it over time. The first step in any scripting process must be to write it out in full. I am amazed at how many people fight scripting however they possess great scripting, they just have failed to write it out, and because of this their skills diminish over time and they have no way to check back and figure out what they are doing differently.

Belief in the message is the single biggest key in the success of any script
Ever wonder why some scripts work and others don't. Or how one person has amazing success saying something but it just doesn't work for you? Well it all comes down to believing in what you say. Belief in the Message; it is so important that it is my Tagline on my blog. People want to listen to someone who speaks with passion and sincerity, not a automaton that can easily spit out the "right words". So no matter how

good the script is, if you do not believe 100% in the words on the page, the meaning behind them and that they are in the very best interests of the client, the success rate you will have will be miniscule.

"Short scripts require word precision, long scripts require message precision."
A short script such as a telephone script require word for word accuracy, where as longer presentational style scripts need to allow the flexibility for message to message accountability.

WORD FOR WORD is needed for these short scripts as even the smallest change can have a huge impact on the results of the script. In fact, small words have greater importance than you given them credit for. In most instances the changes from original script to "personal version" involves what the salesperson sees as unimportant changes. They remove "insignificant words" or change them to a "similar" word. As a scriptwriter let me say that the words the salesperson thinks are important usually are not, and the ones they change are the psychological keys to the success of the script. For example picture a script with the following phrase – "It will update you…" and someone changes that to say, "I will send …" these are seemingly harmless changes, but psychologically speaking the message is drastically different. "I vs. It" – One instance is referring to an automated process versus one where the person will perform a duty. For many clients they are afraid to inconvenience someone else and will say no to an offer with I and yes to an offer with It. "Send versus update" – Send can be interpreted as the whole list each time, rather than update which will convey only changes to the list this can get a client to see a dramatic difference in the offer from what they can get themselves. Lastly, removing the word "you". This is the most common and surprising thing I see in "personalized scripts." You and any version of that word is the most important word in any script. The more you can say it without becoming a crazy person the better. Less 'I's' and more 'you's' is a great thing. It lets your client know that you worry about them and their needs far more often than you do for yourself and your needs.

Tracking is 100% necessary in order to improve a script.
Phone Scripts need to be memorized, internalized, and used for a period time where the results are tracked before looking for ways to improve and change them. Learning the scripts to a point where you can self evaluate if you are using them WORD FOR WORD each and every time you are on the phone, only then can we determine what the exact results are for a script. Then we can make MINOR changes one by one over time and see if there are repercussions or improvements. Most script changes result in a worse performance, certainly in the short term since the belief in the new script has not solidified in us yet. Tracking new scripts takes time and patience and too many people make sweeping changes or make changes too often to get a good handle on the exact results. Most script changes should be tracked weekly for a minimum of one month before any level of evaluation on its success or failure can be determined. Also you should only track one script change at a time. You can see just how long and involved it can be to implement fresh changes to a scripting platform. This is one reason why many people find a script and just stick with it, until it doesn't work anymore.

All scripts need to have a Customer Driven Approach or they will not work!
This is one that we hear over and over, but I am amazed how rarely it is actually utilized. "W.I.F.M. (What's in it for me) is the radio station everyone listens to" is practically a mantra of every sales trainer I have ever spoken to… which is a large number by the way. However time and time again I see huge AGENT FIRST scripting mistakes. Right now the largest one I see is asking the lead if they have an agent helping them too soon in the conversation. Far too many people do this right off the bat,

as the first or second question they ask. This question has no benefit to the client and has nothing to do with their purchasing or selling a home. Yes most boards require the agent to ask this … before offering to provide services, but not before we find out some information about the lead.

This is one example, but the problem is rampant. When you have a script written out, examine it and put yourself in the mind of different buyers and ask yourself, could this question offend me, is this the very best way to ask this, do I feel like the agent cares about me or themselves? Do I feel extra or unwanted pressure from this question?

Scripts are our first impression with people most of the time; make them feel like we care about them, first and our self, second and they will want to have more to do with us.

These five truisms have very little to do with the actual words that are said. I have personally used at least four different "other's Scripts" and 1 of my own that I have altered many times. My script was built from the best parts of other scripts and my own testing and improvements over the years, they have worked for people I have trained and for me over the years. However I saw many other people try to do this exact same script with little to no success. It all came down to understanding and respecting the truisms.

Scripting is only as good as the speakers belief in the message, who wrote the words you use doesn't matter as much as do you believe in what they say.

~~~Andy Herrington

A Personal Message from Me!

I have added some Blank Lined Pages in this book; use these to write out these scripts in your own hand. This will help you to memorize them and help you begin to take ownership over the words. When you can do that, you will begin to see a marked improvement over the results you are having from whatever leads you are using.

I hope you use this book as a means to an end. That you will help more people buy and sell homes and that by working with a quality Real Estate Salesperson such as yourself, that your clients will avoid working with some of those people in our industry that are not in it for the right reasons. I know that when used in the right ways, these scripts can help anyone make a difference in their clients lives as well as create a more professional reputation for our amazing industry.

Good luck and remember the key is your "Belief in the Message" that you are sending.

Andy

POWERHOUSE DIALING
PHONE INTRO &
QUESTIONS SCRIPTS

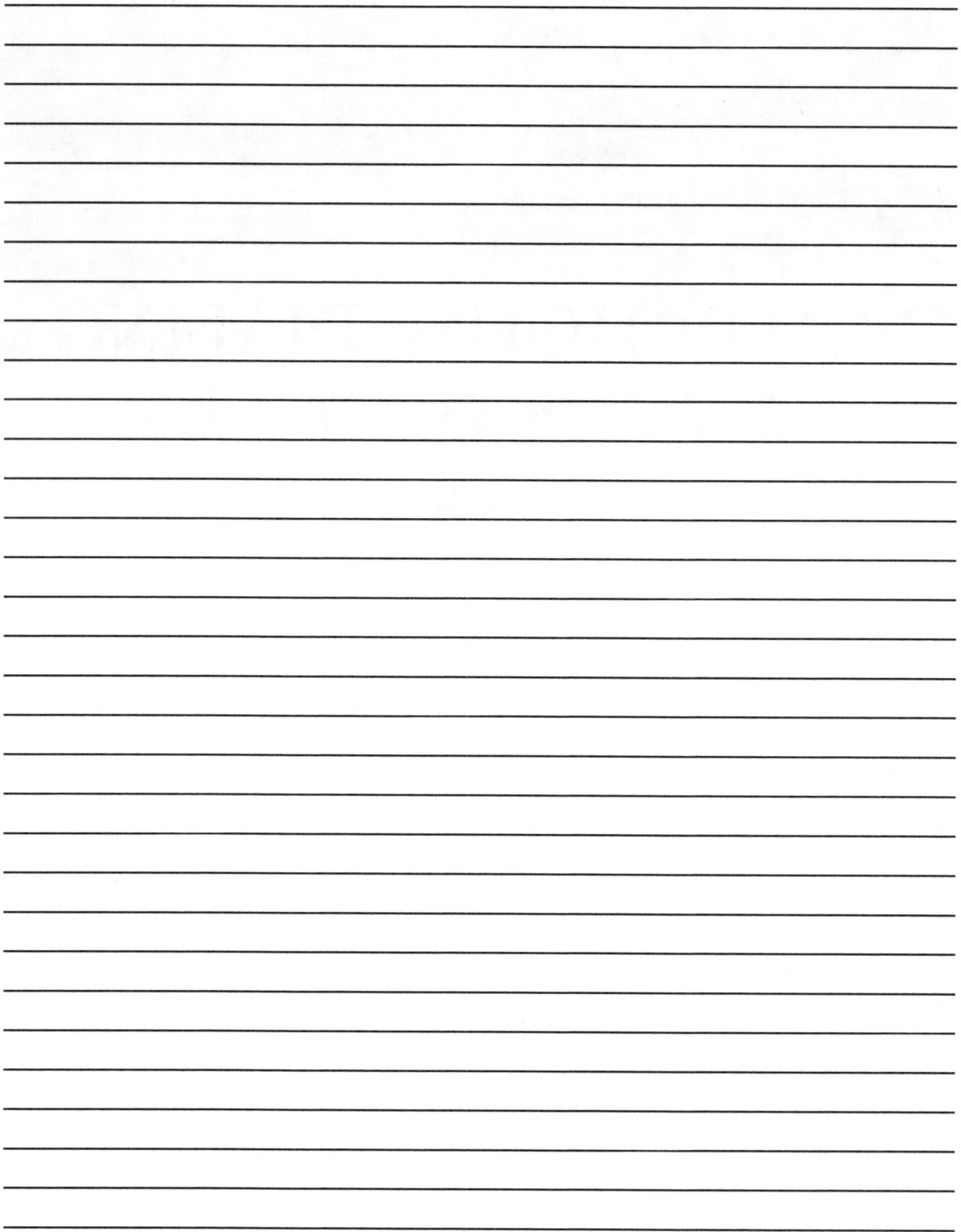

Sign or Ad call INTRO

WHEN THEY CALL US, IT ALLOWS US TO <u>USE PAUSES</u> UNLIKE WHEN WE CALL SOMEONE. A CALLER WILL WAIT PATIENTLY FOR THEIR INFORMATION AND UNDERSTAND SOMEWHAT THAT IT IS NOT IMMEDIATELY AVAILABLE.

Hello this is _____ from _____(eg. Re/Max), how may I help you?

{I'M INTERESTED IN ____AD.}

Excellent, let me take a moment and just pull that up for you. Sorry, who am I speaking with? {Write down their name – also any phone number that may be displayed}

<u>*THEN PAUSE*</u>*, WAIT AT LEAST A COUNT OF "ONE-1000, TWO-1000" THEN CONTINUE, PAUSE BETWEEN EACH QUESTION.*

Sign Ad Call - Questions

Excellent, are you thinking about making a move in the next 3-6 months?

Great, Tell me {NAME}, are you a First time buyer or do you have a house to sell?
(If they have a house to Sell) *Do you want to begin looking for your next home first or get your current home sold first?*

That's exciting (or *That's a Good choice*)**, what methods are you using find your next home?** What they say here is not an objection… YET

And, Do you have an agent in mind to help you through this process?
(IF YES) *Are you 100% committed to that agent or are you open to hearing what additional services I can offer to you?*

Ok, I have that listing up for you – What would you like to know about the property? Give info followed immediately by a question e.g. *299,900 is that in the price range you are looking for? That property is in {area name} is that an area you are hoping for?*

NEXT ACTION:
If not interested in PROPERTY – HEAD TO BUYER OFFER
If INTERESTED in property – HEAD TO SHOWING OFFER

Internet Lead / Long Term Lead INTRO

WE DO NOT HAVE TIME TO SPARE IN THIS CALL. OFFER INFORMATION AND ADVICE- DO NOT TRY TO SELL. THESE ARE PEOPLE WHO ARE EARLY IN THE BUYER PROCESS.

Hello is Jack there please? *(Ask for person who requested information by first name)*

<u>Speak Quickly</u>

Hi Jack this is {salesperson} at {Company Name} I'm calling to let you know that we received <u>your request</u> for copies of {Homes for sale} in {Town Area} and I wanted to let you know that we are preparing that information and will be sending it to you. Is that ok?

Note: Do not ask, "How are you?" You only have a few seconds to get the client to understand that you are calling them back. Try to do this entire paragraph without stopping to breath and at a very quick pace.

Internet/ Long Term Lead - Questions

Excellent, so, how long have you guys been thinking about making a move?

Great, if you did move, where do you hope to end up?

Wow, and when would you like to get this done if everything worked out perfectly?

That's exciting, Are you a first time buyer or do you have a house to sell?

> {Need to know what service the client is looking for}
>
> If they have a house to sell ask:
> *Do you want to begin looking for your next home first or get your current home sold first?*

Do you have an agent in mind to help you through this process?

> B) IF THEY SAY YES ASK:
> *Are you 100% committed to that agent or are you open to hearing what additional services I can offer to you?*

NEXT ACTION: Make a Buyer Value Proposition/ Make a Seller Value Proposition / Make a Follow-up Offer / or Say Goodbye

Instant Text Leads INTRO

Hello this is _____ at _____, we saw that you sent us a text message about one of our listings and I am calling to make sure the system worked properly and sent the correct information out to you, did you receive the information you requested?

Did the information you received answer all of your questions?

If No:

What information were you looking for? (DON"T ANSWER _LOOK UP THE ANSWERS and continue on the SIGN/AD CALL SCRIPT)

If Yes:

NEXT ACTION : QUESTIONS

Instant Text Lead - Questions

Excellent, so, how long have you guys been thinking about making a move?

Great, if you did move, where do you hope to end up?

Wow, and when would you like to get this done if everything worked out perfectly?

That's exciting, Are you a first time buyer or do you have a house to sell?

> If they have a house to sell ask: *Do you want to begin looking for your next home first or get your current home sold first?*

Do you have an agent in mind to help you through this process?

> B) IF THEY SAY YES ASK: *Are you 100% committed to that agent or are you open to hearing what additional services I can offer to you?*

NEXT ACTION: Make a Buyer Value Proposition/ Make a Seller Value Proposition / Make a Follow-up Offer / or Say Goodbye

POWERHOUSE DIALING
BUYER SCRIPTS

Buyer Offer

THIS IS THE STANDARD OFFER FOR ANYONE LOOKING TO BUY A HOME FOR ANY REASON. IT IS VERY HARD TO SAY NO TO. NOT UNTIL THE CLIENT SAYS YES TO THIS OFFER DO WE MOVE ON TO CLOSE FOR AN APPOINTMENT. NOTE WITHOUT AN APPOINTMENT WE DO NOT DO ANYTHING IN THE BUYER OFFER FOR A LEAD. THIS OFFER IS FOR ANY "BUY FIRST", "LOOK FIRST" OR "FIRST TIME BUYER CLIENTS" WE TALK TO.

Offer

Well, what I can do for you is get you daily access to all the information on the homes that match what you're looking for. You will have the address, price and all available photos, all the information just like I get as a Realtor. It will update you instantly by sending out only what is NEW or had a price change, to ensure you have the most up to date information. Oh, and my clients also gain access to bank sales, estate sales and other distress sales, would you be interested in those great deals as well?

Next ACTION – SET the APPOINTMENT

Appointment Setting- Buyer

<u>Booking the Appointment:</u>

Excellent, now all we need to do is meet for about 10-15 min so I can get a handle on what you want in your next home. When is the best time to do this – DAYS, EVENINGS OR WEEKENDS?

Note: We do not ask for permission to meet. Just like a Dentist, Doctor or Lawyer's office – we schedule an appointment.

NEXT ACTION – HANDLE OBJECTIONS OR CONFRIM APPOINTMENT DETAILS

CONFIRM APPOINTMENT
ONCE YOU HAVE THE APPOINTMENT DATE AND TIME WORKED OUT:

Ok, so our appointment is (full date and time e.g. "Tuesday, October 1st at 6pm").

Choose one:

a)   Would you like to come into our office or have me come out to your home?

b)   Do you know where our office is? (if you want appointment at the office only)

c)   I have your address as {123 Primrose} is that correct? (if the have a home to sell)

They respond –

(if they have a home to sell):

After we set you up for the e-mails, would you like me to give you a rough idea on the value of your home in today's market?

Note: we want to say the full date to jog any memory of any other appointments or obstacles that they might have forgotten about.

ALWAYS Finish with:

Excellent, what is going to happen next is that one of my Team Members will give you a call before the appointment. They are going to ask you a few questions so that we can be more prepared for our meeting and ensure we provide you with a quality set of listings to kick-start your home search. Also if you would like to know a little more about us, visit (www. Yoursocialproofsite .com) Other than that we will see you on {appointment date} Thank you.

NEXT ACTION: _Enter notes in your CRM_

Showing Offer

If the Lead wants to view a listing, Book the Appointment – Date and Time First then we will tell them we will meet at the office or their home.

Excellent, so are you interested in seeing only this home, or anything that represents as good a deal as this one?

<u>If only interested in this home:</u>

Why don't we set up a time to view this property, what works best for you … days, evenings or weekends? (Set date and time)

NEXT ACTION – Confirm Appointment

<u>If interested in anything that represents as good a deal:</u>

<u>NEXT ACTION-*HEAD TO BUYER OFFER*</u>

TOP 5 Appointment Objections

THESE OBJECTION HANDLES NEED TO BE POSTED ANYWHERE YOU HANDLE CALLS. THE KEY TO HANDLING ANY OBJECTION IS TO SOLVE THEIR OBJECTION WITH A BENEFIT TO THEM. MAKE THEM COMFORTABLE AND THEY WILL MEET. THESE ARE THE MOST COMMON AND COME AFTER WE HAVE ATTEMPTED TO BOOK AN APPOINTMENT.

I don't have time to meet:

You know this was created for a busy person like you. Sending all the information to your e-mail makes it so you can check it whenever you have time. Plus it will save you more time simply because you will have complete access to the information about the homes that interest you. It takes 10-15 min now but will save you hours and hours during the process of looking for your next home; what is better for you Days, Evenings or Weekends?

Can't we just meet at the house? (SHOWING OBJECTION)

I'm sorry but my agreement with this seller is that I will not show the property to a client I have not met before. I'm sure you can understand that. It only takes 10-15 minutes and then we will head over to see the house. Also, If you want, we can go computer shopping, LIVE on my realtor exclusive website and I'll even attempt to book appointments for us the same day on any homes you see on the computer. So do you know where our office is?

<u>Just send me the emails, I can tell you right now what I want:</u>

I know that you know exactly what you are looking for in your next home, and in order to do a great job for you; I need to understand your needs fully too. I'm going to sit down and take the proper time to get a firm grasp of what you want, this way I don't waste your time by sending you hundreds of homes that don't match what you are looking for or worse than that, miss out on that <u>great</u> deal, it only takes 10-15 min and then we are on our way to finding you your next home; what is better for you Days, Evenings or Weekends?

<u>I'm already getting that info online:</u>

The Internet is a great place to start your home search. The problem is that it is usually behind, often by weeks or months, and as I'm sure you are aware, the good deals go quickly! What I'm offering to you now is far superior, I will get you access to all the real estate information just like a realtor gets. What you are going to receive will update you daily what is new on the market or had a price change, so you are one of the first people to know about the great deals. It only takes 10-15 min and then we are on our way to finding you your next home; what is better for you Days, Evenings or Weekends?

<u>I need to check with my spouse:</u>

Well, that's a great idea, let's do this... we will set a tentative time that normally works for you and your spouse a few days from now, then you can speak with them and I'll give you a call the day before to confirm that it still works for the both of you; no one will show up without us speaking again, so what <u>usually</u> works best for your spouse, Days, Evenings or Weekends?

Top 5 Information Objections

THESE OBJECTION HANDLES NEED TO BE POSTED ANYWHERE YOU HANDLE CALLS. THE KEY TO HANDLING ANY OBJECTION IS TO SOLVE THEIR OBJECTION WITH A BENEFIT TO THEM. MAKE THEM COMFORTABLE AND THEY WILL MEET. THESE OBJECTIONS WILL COME EARLIER IN THE CALL, OFTEN AFTER THE BUYER OFFER. BE READY TO HANDLE THEM.

I'm not really sure what I'm looking for (Not ready yet):

You know, that is very common. What I do with people in this situation is set up an email search to help them gain Market Knowledge. Everyone loves the information and it helps them make a quality decision, sometimes that is to buy and sometimes that is to do nothing at all. Either way, you know you are making a quality decision using all of the information available. Also, with this plan, you will know immediately if a great deal comes along. Can you see how this will help you with your home search?

What is better for you Days, Evenings or Weekends?

I don't want to waste your time:

I appreciate that, but please understand that this is what I do. I help people make quality decisions about Real Estate. Sometimes that is to buy, and sometimes it is to do nothing at all. I never consider it to be a waste of my time to help people. This is just the way I do things. I know that my list of homes will help you make a quality decision; can you see how this will help you with your home search?

What is better for you Days, Evenings or Weekends?

<u>(Point 2Agent.com / you / your website) set me up already for the emails: (if you have a service like this)</u>

That's a great place to start, what you have signed up for includes my listings and those that others have allowed me to send. What I'm offering to you now is far superior; I will get you access to all the real estate information just like I get as a realtor. What you are going to receive will update you daily what is new on the market or had a price change, so you are one of the first people to know about the great deals. It only takes 10-15 min and then we are on our way to finding you your next home; what is better for you Days, Evenings or Weekends?

<u>I'm getting that info from newspapers and magazines:</u>

That's a great way to get familiar with the market. The problem is the fact that newspaper & magazine deadlines are at least 1 week before print and often have a long shelf life. What I'm offering to you now is far superior; I will get you access to all the real estate information just like I get as a realtor. What you are going to receive will update you daily what is new on the market or had a price change, so you are one of the first people to know about the great deals. It only takes 10-15 min and then we are on our way to finding you your next home; what is better for you Days, Evenings or Weekends?

I simply drive by the areas I want; I know which streets I want:

So you really know the exact area you are looking for, that's great. Are you aware that only about 84% of homeowners actually want a sign on their lawn, and that it can take 48-72 hours just to get the sign installed. What I'm offering to you now is far superior; I will get you access to all the real estate information just like I get as a realtor. What you are going to receive will update you daily what is new on the market or had a price change, so you are one of the first people to know about the great deals. It only takes 10-15 min and then we are on our way to finding you your next home; what is better for you Days, Evenings or Weekends?

Other Buyer Objections

THESE OBJECTION HANDLES NEED TO BE POSTED ANYWHERE YOU HANDLE CALLS. THE KEY TO HANDLING ANY OBJECTION IS TO SOLVE THEIR OBJECTION WITH A BENEFIT TO THEM. MAKE THEM COMFORTABLE AND THEY WILL MEET. THE FOLLOWING OBJECTIONS ARE MORE RARE, BUT DO OCCUR. REMEMBER THE GOAL OF THE CALL IS TO BOOK A FACE-TO-FACE APPOINTMENT, NOT TO CONVINCE THE CALLER TO WORK WITH US.

<u>I'm not going to sign anything!</u>

I understand. *You* don't have to sign a thing. We are just going to get you the information you need to make a quality Real Estate decision. What is best for you Days, Evenings or Weekends?

<u>I only want to deal with listing agents:</u> *Prove their reasoning wrong with Logic questions!*

OK, and Why are you looking at doing that?

<u>To save commission:</u>

So you feel that the homeowner will sell their home for less than market value to you?

<u>Yes:</u>

Why would they do that?

<u>To save money:</u>

So they will save money and you will save money?

<u>Yes:</u>

So really how much money do you expect to save?

<u>$$$$</u>

Don't you think that a Buyer agent – working solely on your behalf, doing a quality job could negotiate that amount and more for you, especially when if they don't they will not get paid at all?

<u>Do you deal with Rental properties? / I think I'll just rent for now: (if you don't do rentals)</u>

Are you hoping to buy a home after that?

<u>If "Yes":</u>

When do you hope to make a purchase if everything works out perfectly?

(Depending on their answer decide if you will Make an Offer, Book a follow-up or Say goodbye. You may have to help them rent a property now, then buy in a few months, but this simple question can add a few deals to your business every year.)

<u>If "No I can't afford it":</u>

Ok well, you see most Rental properties don't go through the Real Estate Agents, they just get listed in the paper, I would suggest you try that route for awhile and see if you can't find a unit. If you need us in the future, don't hesitate to call, Have a Good Day.

<u>I don't have an Email Address:</u>

That's okay, I can maybe be of even more help then, I will set up our e-mail search for you but instead of sending you the e-mails, I will send them to myself. This way we are still looking on a Daily Basis, and then I will call you with any homes that I know would you will be interested in and set up the showings. Would you be interested in that?

Follow-up Offers

NOT ALL CALLS WILL END IN AN APPOINTMENT SO HOW DO WE GET OFF THE PHONE? WELL IN 97% OF THE TIME, WE SHOULD WANT TO BE CALLING THIS PERSON BACK. WE WILL TELL THEM WE ARE CALLING AGAIN, BUT ASK THEM WHEN WE SHOULD DO IT.

Buyer Follow-up Offer

When you have done all you can for the lead for now but you want to speak to them again, set up a follow-up call.

Well (Name) we love to keep in touch with our clients, when do think would be the best time for me to follow up with you?

(Don't ask can I call you back, just ask when!)

Excellent, also if you want to know a little more about us please visit (<u>www.socialproofsite.com</u>). Thank you for your time today. Good bye.

Appointment Reminder Call

NOW THAT WE HAVE BOOKED AN APPOINTMENT, THE NEXT BIG CHALLENGE IS ACTUALLY GETTING THE CLIENT TO SHOW UP. TO HELP IMPROVE THE PERCENTAGES, USE A REMINDER CALL. A CALL THAT DOES NOT SIMPLY CONFIRM THE APPOINTMENT DATE AND TIME, BUT REMINDS THE CLIENT OF THE BENEFITS AND THE REASONS THEY BOOKED THE APPOINTMENT IN THE FIRST PLACE.

KNOWING THIS WE NEED A SCRIPT TO REMIND THE CLIENT ABOUT WHAT WE ARE DOING AT THE APPOINTMENT, REINVIGORATE THEIR EXCITEMENT LEVEL AND REMIND THEM WHEN AND WHERE THE APPOINTMENT IS. WE NEED TO TRY A COUPLE OF TIMES TO SPEAK TO THE CLIENT ON THE PHONE, HOWEVER, THIS IS ONE TIME WHERE LEAVING A MESSAGE IS OK AS WELL.

IT NEEDS TO BE DONE THE NIGHT BEFORE THE APPOINTMENT OR THE MORNING OF THE APPOINTMENT AT THE VERY LATEST.

LIKE IN ANYTHING THIS IS NOT A FOOLPROOF SOLUTION BUT WILL INCREASE YOUR FACE-TO-FACE APPOINTMENTS.

THIS IS A ONE SIDED SCRIPT; WE WANT OUR EXCITEMENT TO BE BURSTING THROUGH AND GET THEM MOTIVATED TO SEE US. I DON'T REALLY WANT THEM TO SPEAK AT ALL IF POSSIBLE. LEAD THEM!

Buyer Appointment Reminder Call Script

Hi {name} this is (agent) calling from (company). I wanted to let you know that I've gotten some great things organized for our appointment. I know you are going to be excited by what is available for you right now.

So we are meeting tomorrow at (TIME) at (LOCATION) and I can't wait to meet you and get you this great information to kick-start your home search.

Plus I know you will be really happy receiving the daily updates that include the Estate Sales, power of sales and other distressed properties. This way you will never miss out on a great deal.

Ok, as you can tell, I am really excited about helping you find a great deal on your next home. I look forward to seeing you tomorrow.

If you need to reach me, my cell number is ...

This can be used as a Voice mail as well, but attempt to reach the client at least twice before leaving the message.

POWERHOUSE DIALING
SELLER SCRIPTS

Seller Offer

HERE ARE THE OFFERS YOU CAN MAKE TO A SELLING CLIENT; THERE ARE LESS OBJECTIONS BECAUSE SELLERS KNOW THEY NEED TO MEET WITH AN AGENT TO LIST THEIR HOME.

Seller Offer

Well, what I can do for you is give you a Full Marketplace Evaluation on your house in today's market. We can also discuss what the right time to put your house up for sale is, and the costs that are involved so you know exactly what to expect. Oh and my clients also get access to some innovative ideas that on average increase the selling price of your home by about 5%. Would you be interested in those as well?

NEXT   ACTION   :   Setting   the   Appointment

Appointment Booking- Seller

Booking the Appointment:

All we need to do now is book at time for us to come over, when is the best time for you, DAYS, EVENINGS OR WEEKENDS.

BOOK DATE and TIME and AGENT

NEXT ACTION: Confirm Appointment

CONFIRM APPOINTMENT

<u>ONCE YOU HAVE THE APPOINTMENT DATE AND TIME WORKED OUT:</u>

Ok, so our appointment is (full date and time e.g. "Tuesday, October 1ˢᵗ at 6pm with {agent's name}. And to confirm your address is {123 Primrose St in Whitby} is this correct?

<u>They Respond</u>

Excellent, what is going to happen next is that one of our Team Members will give you a call before the appointment. They are going to ask you a few questions so that we can be more prepared for our meeting and ensure we provide you with a quality evaluation for your house. Also If you would like to know a little more about us, visit (<u>www.socialproofsite.com</u>) Other than that we will see you on {appointment date} Thank you.

This allows the agent to call back and go through a pre-determined Checklist of information about the home so they can build rapport and get better info for a CMA as needed.

Top 3 Seller Objections

THESE OBJECTIONS ARE MORE RARE AS THE CLIENT KNOWS AN AGENT NEEDS TO COME OVER, BUT THEY STILL DO EXIST. REMEMBER THAT THE GOAL IS THE APPOINTMENT, NOT CONVINCING THEM TO WORK WITH US.

<u>What Commission do you charge? (Most popular Objection)</u>

Well, with us, you are in control of that, we have a few service packages available ranging from 3.5% to 7% commission. We will explain them all to you and you will choose which service you would like. When is the best time for us to come over, Days, Evenings or Weekends?

<u>I can't book without talking to my spouse/ other:</u>

Well, that's a great idea, let's do this ... we will set a tentative time that normally works for you and your spouse a few days from now, then you can speak with them and I'll give you a call the day before to confirm that it still works for the both of you; no one will show up without us speaking again, so what <u>usually</u> works best for your spouse, Days, Evenings or Weekends?

<u>I don't know when I'll be available. / I don't have any time. / I'm simply too busy right now to meet:</u>

I understand everyone is very busy these days; this is why we work 9am to 10pm, 7 days a week. We take less than an hour and it is a free of charge, no obligation evaluation. Once this is done, we will do everything else, what time would it be best for us to come by?

Other Seller Objections

<u>Can you send me an evaluation by email?</u>
I can send you an email with a rough idea on value. However, in order to do an accurate job for you, we need to see your home. As I'm sure you are aware, the inside of your home affects the value a great deal. It takes less than an hour and we also give you those tips that on average improve the value of your home by about 5%; what's better for you, Days, Evenings or Weekends?

<u>I already know the value of my home:</u>
That's great, would you also like to learn some low-cost ways to raise the value of your home by about 5%? Also we can show you some innovative techniques to get your home sold in the least amount of time. Would you be interested in that information as well?

Follow-up Offers

NOT ALL CALLS WILL END IN AN APPOINTMENT SO HOW DO WE GET OFF THE PHONE? WELL IN 97% OF THE TIMES, WE SHOULD WANT TO BE CALLING THIS PERSON BACK. WE WILL TELL THEM WE ARE CALLING AGAIN, BUT ASK THEM WHEN WE SHOULD DO IT.

Seller Follow-up

This is used to set up a follow up call with a lead that is not ready to list their home and is not interested in any Buyer information.

What I can do for you is send you a quick email with everything that has been listed or sold in your area in the last little while. It will include the addresses, pictures and price so you can compare them to your home. This will give you a rough idea of what your home is worth in today's market. Then when you are closer to listing we will come out and give you a much more accurate evaluation at that time. How does that sound?

Excellent, (Name) we love to keep in touch with our clients, when do think would be the best time for me to follow up with you?

Great, also if you want to know a little more about us please visit (<u>www.socialproofsite.com</u>). Thank you for your time today. Good-bye.

Appointment Reminder Call

NOW THAT WE HAVE BOOKED AN APPOINTMENT, THE NEXT BIG CHALLENGE IS ACTUALLY GETTING THE CLIENT TO SHOW UP. TO HELP IMPROVE THE PERCENTAGES, USE A REMINDER CALL. A CALL THAT DOES NOT SIMPLY CONFIRM THE APPOINTMENT DATE AND TIME, BUT REMINDS THE CLIENT OF THE BENEFITS AND THE REASONS THEY BOOKED THE APPOINTMENT IN THE FIRST PLACE.

KNOWING THIS WE NEED A SCRIPT TO REMIND THE CLIENT ABOUT WHAT WE ARE DOING AT THE APPOINTMENT, REINVIGORATE THEIR EXCITEMENT LEVEL AND REMIND THEM WHEN AND WHERE THE APPOINTMENT IS. WE NEED TO TRY A COUPLE OF TIMES TO SPEAK TO THE CLIENT ON THE PHONE, HOWEVER, THIS IS ONE TIME WHERE LEAVING A MESSAGE IS OK AS WELL.

IT NEEDS TO BE DONE THE NIGHT BEFORE THE APPOINTMENT OR THE MORNING OF THE APPOINTMENT AT THE VERY LATEST.

LIKE IN ANYTHING THIS IS NOT A FOOLPROOF SOLUTION BUT WILL INCREASE YOUR FACE-TO-FACE APPOINTMENTS.

THIS IS A ONE SIDED SCRIPT; WE WANT OUR EXCITEMENT TO BE BURSTING THROUGH AND GET THEM MOTIVATED TO SEE US. I DON'T REALLY WANT THEM TO SPEAK AT ALL IF POSSIBLE. LEAD THEM!

Seller Appointment Reminder Call Script

Hi {name} this is (agent) calling from (company or Team/Company). I wanted to let you know that I've gotten some great things organized for our appointment. I know you are going to be pleased about what the Marketplace says about the value of your home.

So we are meeting tomorrow at (TIME) at (LOCATION) and I can't wait to meet you and get you this great information so we can begin the process of getting you Top Dollar for your home.

Plus I know you will be really happy about the marketing plans we have and the commission structures for you to choose from.

Ok, as you can tell, I am really excited about helping you get your Home Sold. I look forward to seeing you tomorrow.

If you need to reach me, my cell number is …

This can be used as a Voice mail as well, but attempt to reach the client at least twice before leaving the message.

COI / Past Client Referral script

USE THIS SCRIPT TO GENERATE AN ABUNDANCE OF REPEAT AND REFERRAL BUSINESS!

Hello is (NAME) there please? (Ask for First name of the person you know)

Hi (NAME) this is (agent's name) how are you doing. HAVE A BRIEF CHAT ABOUT LIFE IN GENERAL. (E.g. Last time we spoke you…) THEN FOLLOW UP WITH…

I know it has been awhile since we talked about business and I would like to believe that if given the chance, you would recommend me to your family and friends, am I right to believe this?

{USUALLY – YA SURE,}

Thank you, I also talk to many new people every day, and when I see a need, I always try to refer to my past clients, friends and family as well. What I realized is I have no idea how to know when someone I talk to might need you or your company's services unless they are especially blunt about it. So I wanted to ask you so I would know in the future. What should I look for (NAME)?

{Listen take notes}

Ok I am going to pay attention for that (if you have anyone refer right now). *Then Continue…*

Do you mind if I give you a few things to look for as well, because rarely will people be straightforward and say, "I need a Real Estate Agent."

{USUALLY sure go ahead}

OK so most people need Real Estate services before, during or after a big life event. So what will happen is you will hear people talk about becoming pregnant, getting engaged, Getting separated, Getting a raise at work, or a possible job transfer, even a downsizing. Kids going off to high school or university soon are other big ones. These are the sorts of things to look for. When this happens, you can do a couple of things, you can ask them are they thinking about making a move and work towards a referral, however most of my friends simply make a mental note to pass on their contact info to me so I can contact them. I can do this as discreetly as you desire. And I really appreciate any referrals you can pass my way.

Now that we have that settled, do you know of anyone that might need my services any time soon?

{Usually no one comes to mind}

No problem, thank you for thinking about me, I really appreciate it. I'm going to touch base with you regarding this periodically if that is OK with you. Thanks a lot (Name). I'll talk to you soon hopefully with a referral for you.

Canadian Expired Script A / Cold Call

THIS SCRIPT IS FOR THE SITUATION WHERE YOU CANNOT KNOW THE EXPIRED LISTING HAS EXPIRED. WE CALL THE STREET AROUND THE EXPIRED WITH THIS "COLD CALL" STYLE SCRIPT THEN HANDLE THE EXPIRED OBJECTION WHEN THEY TELL US.

Hello is {Mr. or Mrs. Last name} there please?

Hi {Mr. or Mrs. Last name} this is {salesperson} from {Company or TEAM at Company}. I'm calling to let you know that we have begun a strong marketing campaign in your area. As I'm sure you are aware {The Super Awesome Team} is one of the top sales teams in the area, and we are now looking to focus our efforts in your community. I'm simply calling to find out are you planning on making a move in the next 3 to 6 months?

If you do move do you plan on staying in (*town*) or moving out of (*town*)?

Do you have an agent in mind to help you with your move?

When do you hope to get this done if everything worked out perfectly?

Do you want to look for your next home first or get your current home sold first?

NEXT ACTION: *Make an Offer / Or Set a Follow-up / Or Say Good bye!*

Canadian Expired Script B / Cold Call

THIS SCRIPT IS FOR THE SITUATION WHERE YOU CANNOT KNOW THE EXPIRED LISTING HAS EXPIRED. WE CALL THE STREET AROUND THE EXPIRED WITH THIS "COLD CALL" STYLE SCRIPT THEN HANDLE THE EXPIRED OBJECTION WHEN THEY TELL US.

Hello is {Mr. or Mrs. Last name} there please?

Hi {Mr. or Mrs. Last name} this is {salesperson} from {Company or TEAM at Company}. The reason I'm calling is because we are offering your neighbourhood Free Market Evaluations to help you and other homeowners understand what your home is worth in Today's challenging market. Would you be interested in receiving a Free no obligation home evaluation from one of the Top Sales People in the {area name}?

[If yes, I don't know or Maybe, Jump to Seller Offer.]

Common reaction is you're the 400th Real Estate agent to call me today. My home just expired, don't you know.

Once they tell you they expired.

Oh really, you know a lot of people are in that situation in this (tough...) market, out of curiosity, why do you think your Home didn't Sell?

{THEN SHUT UP and listen closely, you need to handle the objection, also Don't be afraid to look toward the Buying side here, it will calm the expired vendor some, as it seems you are looking for their interests then come back to the expiry}

That's a shame, you know, in today's market the Real Estate Board stats show that only about xx% (45-55-60??) of listings are selling, did your last agent tell you that?
Would you like to hear how we sell 96% of our listings, and how we do it in less time and for more money than the average realtor?

{Or give the Standard Seller offer.}

<u>Also the Hail Mary Pass when they are leaving us without booking an appointment:</u>

Oh, well in that case, I have a Fantastic Step by Step Independent Guide that explains the reasons why a home hasn't sold and How to go about selling a house that didn't sell. I would be more than happy to have it delivered to you free of charge; all I ask in return is that you accept my business card with the package. How does that sound?

[You can find these on www.about.com.]

COI- TEAM - New Agent on a File Call

THIS SCRIPT IS FOR TEAMS ONLY, SPECIFICALLY THE SITUATION WHERE WE ARE CHANGING THE AGENT WHO IS LOOKING AFTER THE CLIENT.

Is {Client name} there?

Hi {name} it's {Agent Name} from the _____ Team at _____. I am calling to let you know that I have been assigned your file and will be your contact person with the Team from now on.

"Share a piece of information – Home values, sales in area…"

So, how are things going with any current real estate plans?

POWERHOUSE DIALING
ROLE-PLAY

RULES FOR ROLE-PLAY

1.   Role-play is practice; make sure you treat the caller as you would a real client. "Oh I wouldn't normally do _____" is not a valid excuse.

2.   Have a pen and paper with you and take notes like it is a real call.

3.   No talking unless you are a part of the role-play, Listen carefully and be ready to provide helpful critique.

4.   When giving your constructive criticism remember to use the "compliment then criticize" strategy.

5.   Role-play is a learning environment, be open to all comments and suggestions. Everyone is just trying to help you make more money!

6.   When being a caller/client remember to follow the scenario for your client, but always have the mindset that you will do what the Agent is asking you to do (e.g. Meet, list your home, sign a contract). We will get enough practice not booking appointments in the real world.

7.   Remember, objections are great but too many and a caller is just being difficult.

8.   As a client you will be given a fair bit of circumstantial info, not all of it needs to come out in the role-play.

9.   As an agent you do not have to book every single appointment, only the ones you want to attend.

10.   Be confident, and energetic. Practice your mirror and matching, and try to pick out the different personality types.

ROLE-PLAY SAMPLE SCENARIOS

AD CALL
123 PRIMROSE AVE
LOCAL LISTING
$_____
2 STORY, 4 BED CORNER LOT.

Client   *Billy*   *Ratner:*

You are a Buy first person looking to upsize and move into town. Want 4 Bed 2.5 bath, decent yard detached, and 300-400 in price. You have a home to sell in the "country" it is bungalow 2 bed 1400 sq. ft. 1.3 acre. You are not worried about your home selling. If agent pushes too hard about seeing your home you will get turned off completely and become much more determined to meet at the house, Calling the agent on the fact that they only want to list your home. At this point the Appoint is very unlikely unless the meet your criteria. You would prefer see the home you called in on no matter what, you will prefer to meet at the home, it is right near where you work. If not convinced as to why you can't meet at the home, a little annoyed, "I don't see why we can't do this the other agents have been willing to"

AD CALL
123 PRIMROSE AVE
OUT OF AREA (LOSS LEADER AD)
$_____
2 STORY, 4 BED CORNER LOT.

Client: *Max*   *Waxman:*

You are a guy who has been looking to buy for a little while you are afraid of agents and are a little concerned about "Getting Taken" by a slick talker. Your fallbacks are "I'm just looking" "Not sure when I will doing anything" very Non Committal on the phone. You will run quickly if attacked in your mind. If the questions asked seem invasive or aggressive. You are not afraid to lie or push back if pushed. "That is none of your business" However, you are Pre- app'd by the bank, and have a good job, great credit and a healthy Down Payment. You would be interested in Emails, but would run from appointment, Too busy, can get this info on the Internet. If convinced would meet, if put at ease you would be easily swayed in fact.

AD CALL
123 PRIMROSE AVE
LOCAL LISTING
$_____
2 STORY, 3 BED TOWN.

Client:	Alex	Findley:

You are looking around for a home in Local area. Looking to downsize into a town home, because you are divorced. You bought wife out 3 years ago, and are selling the home now. You know that you need to Sell first, but have no real idea how to go about it. You want an idea of what is on the market since another agent has given you a value on your home. You are happy with that value and are just seeing what is out there and getting home ready for sale. If the agent doesn't offer **SOMETHING OF VALUE** *to you (how "we" are different is not something of value), you will not meet. You will list with the other agent unless convinced otherwise.*

INTERNET LEAD
LOCAL LISTINGS
$_____
2 STORY, 3 BED TOWN.

Client: **Brad**   **Lennox:**

You just started looking around for a home in Local area. Looking to buy first home with your soon to be wife. You are getting married in 3 months. You are excited but worried you don't have time to buy before the wedding. You are really new to real estate and have done nothing but look online for a couple of days.

INTERNET LEAD
LOCAL LISTINGS
$_____
2 STORY, 4 BED, POOL

Client: *Wendy*   *Macintyre:*

You just started looking around for a home in Local area. You have a home to sell but don't care about selling it, need to find your dream home first. Hubby will do what you tell him, but doesn't know you are thinking about this. Want a pool for the kids as they transition to high school. Want to be in the same area. No real idea on value of home or the market.

INTERNET LEAD
LOCAL LISTINGS
$_____
BUNGALOW WITH LAND

Client: *Justin*   *Petterson:*

You just started looking around for a home in Local area. You and your Boyfriend have dreams of buying a hobby farm in the local area. Unrealistic on price, but honestly you NEED to buy something to live together soon. Both have good jobs but no pre-approval. You are a very energetic person with a lot to say and strong opinions. You just want information ASAP so you can move things along

INTERNET LEAD
LOCAL LISTINGS
$_____
2 STORY, 5 BED DETACHED WITH 3 CAR
GARAGE OR WORKSHOP

Client: *Jessica*   *Morris:*

You just started looking around for a home in Local area. You live in the bad part of town, grew up there too. You sound uneducated and you enjoy the booze and dope. You and your common law biker boyfriend are looking to move up in the world. He has lots of money but you keep that on the down low. You literally could buy the house with cash if you wanted to but would never tell anyone that especially over the phone. No pre-approval, you do not have a job.

TEXT LEAD
123 PRIMROSE RD
LOCAL LISTING
$_____
2 STORY, 3 BED TOWN.

Client: *Barry*   *Snow:*

You drove by the listing and sent a text to get info. You did this because you assumed you would not talk to a real estate agent. They scare you. You are not pre-approved, and are afraid of the bank. You really want to buy but the process scares you because you don't know what to expect. You don't want to have people waste time on you because you know you don't make decisions.

TEXT LEAD
123 PRIMROSE RD
LOCAL LISTING
$_____
4 BED BUNGALOW ON MATURE STREET

Client: *Mindy*   *Merrick:*

You drove by the listing and sent a text to get info. You absolutely love this house and it is your dream home, you want to get as much info about it without given any info back if possible. You have a home to sell and would have the agent come to give you a value but not until you saw inside that home. You cannot afford this house, but need to move up any way. You are pregnant and a little crazy with the emotions from time to time. If the agent says anything "wrong" you would react poorly quickly.

ABOUT THE AUTHOR

Andy Herrington is a Canadian Real Estate Salesperson, International Author, High Energy Speaker and Real Estate Business Coach. He was a part of 3 of the Top Real Estate Sales Teams on Canada's Largest Real Estate Board. For 6 Years, he was an active member and manager for the different team's Inside Sales Teams as a Phone Specialist. During this stretch these teams averaged over 350 sales a year, and completed in excess of 2100 deals. In 4 of those 6 years the team he was on ranked #1 on Canada's Largest Real estate Board, the Toronto Real Estate Board for Units sold or Volume of sales.

Andy went on to be the Director of Coaching and a Master Coach for the first "Team Specific" training company Dan Plowman Team Systems. He stayed there for 4 years, before branching off on his own to develop and build Powerhouse Coaching. This allowed Andy the freedom to use all of the knowledge from all of the teams he has been a part of either as Team Member or as a Master Coach.

Over the years Andy has coached 7 of the Top 15 Producers in the Toronto Real Estate Board, as well as the Top Producer in 5 other Canadian Real Estate Boards. Andy has helped Real Estate Salespeople all across Canada strive to do better and make the Industry a more professional place.

Andy has had numerous articles published internationally as well as in Canada, most notably in SOLD Magazine and REM magazine. He runs a blog @ andyherrington.com and can be seen at speaking engagements across North America.

Lastly To inquire about having Andy speak to your team or brokerage or have Andy as your coach, or your teams coach contact him directly @ andy@andyherrington.com, you will not be disappointed.

www.ingramcontent.com/pod-product-compliance
Lightning Source LLC
Chambersburg PA
CBHW082108210326
41599CB00033B/6628